SUMMER MATH WORKBOOK

Bridge Building Activities

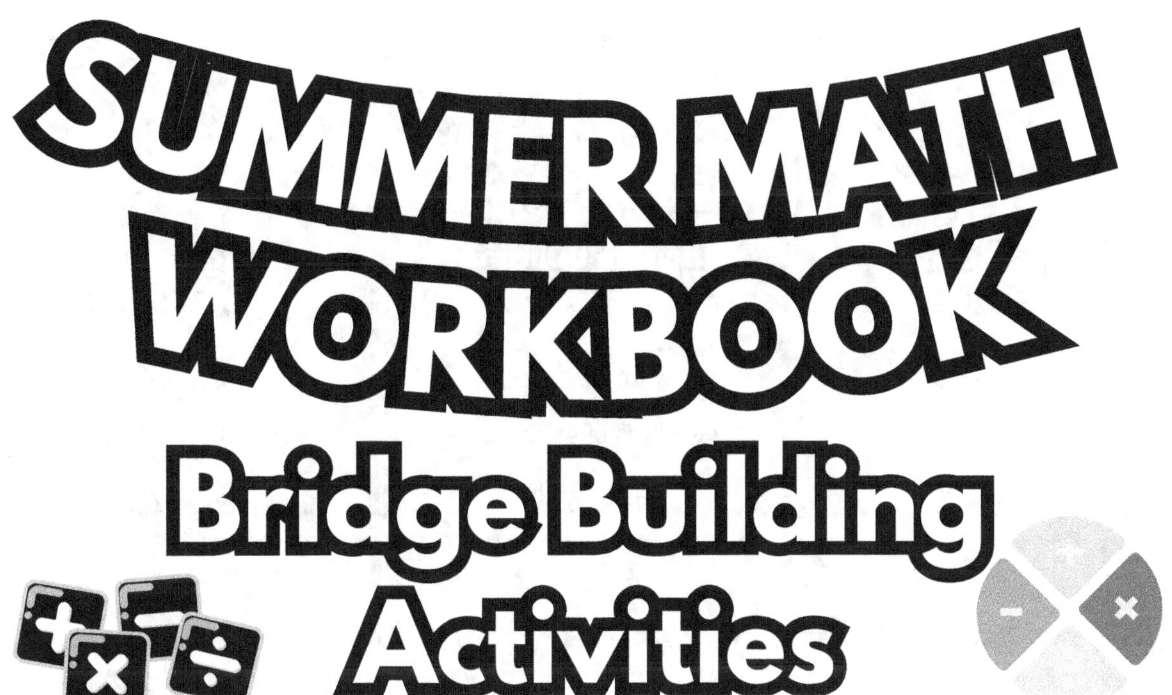

Grade
1 → 2
SUMMER MATH WORKBOOK
Bridge Building Activities
Number Sense
Addition and Subtraction
Place Value

Grade
2 → 3
SUMMER MATH WORKBOOK
Bridge Building Activities
Number Sense
Addition and Subtraction
Place Value

Grade
3 → 4
SUMMER MATH WORKBOOK
Bridge Building Activities
Number Sense
Addition and Subtraction
Place Value

Grade
4 → 5
SUMMER MATH WORKBOOK
Bridge Building Activities
Multiplication and Division
Place Value and Units
Fractions and Geometry

Grade
5 → 6
SUMMER MATH WORKBOOK
Bridge Building Activities
Multiplication and Division
Factors and Multiples
Fractions and Geometry

Grade
6 → 7
SUMMER MATH WORKBOOK
Bridge Building Activities
Arithmetic
Algebra
Geometry and Statistics

Grade
7 → 8
SUMMER MATH WORKBOOK
Bridge Building Activities
Ratio and Percentage
Algebra and Cartesian Plane
Geometry and Statistics

Grade
8 → 9
SUMMER MATH WORKBOOK
Bridge Building Activities
Ratio and Percentage
Algebra
Geometry and Graphing

Grade
9 → 10
SUMMER MATH WORKBOOK
Bridge Building Activities
Factoring and Distributing
Algebra
Geometry and Graphing

<u>Introduction</u>

As parents and educators, we understand the pivotal role that mathematics plays in shaping a child's academic journey and future success. Yet, the path to mathematical proficiency can often seem daunting, filled with challenges and complexities. That's where the transformative power of Summer Bridge Building Activities books comes into play, illuminating the way forward with clarity, precision, and purpose.

Summer vacation is a time for rest and relaxation, but it also presents the risk of the "summer slide," where students lose some of the academic gains they made during the school year. Summer Bridge Building Activities books are specifically designed to tackle this challenge, ensuring that your child stays academically engaged and prepared for the upcoming school year. These books provide a seamless bridge from one grade to the next, reinforcing essential skills and introducing new concepts that will give your child a head start.

Imagine your child eagerly diving into the pages of a Summer Bridge Building Activities book, greeted by clear, engaging content that demystifies complex mathematical concepts. With each turn of the pages, they embark on a journey of discovery, encountering thoughtfully curated practice questions that reinforce learning and sharpen problem-solving skills. As they unveil the answers to those questions, a sense of accomplishment blossoms within them — a tangible reward for their hard work and dedication.

Summer Bridge Building Activities books transcend traditional educational tools; they are meticulously crafted to build a deep and enduring understanding of mathematics. These books follow a sequential and logical progression, starting from fundamental principles and advancing to sophisticated problem-solving strategies. Each chapter is designed to build on the previous one, ensuring a solid and comprehensive foundation for future learning.

Parents, we yearn for nothing more than to see our children thrive academically and personally. We want to witness the spark of inspiration ignited within them as they overcome academic challenges with confidence and poise. Summer Bridge Building Activities books serve as indispensable partners in this noble endeavor, offering not just practice questions but the keys to unlocking a world of academic and personal opportunities.

Visualize the pride on your child's face as they master a challenging math concept, the joy they experience when their efforts yield results, and the confidence they gain with each success. These pages are designed to make learning math a positive, enriching, and deeply rewarding experience that will benefit them throughout their academic journey and beyond.

For educators, Summer Bridge Building Activities books are invaluable allies in the quest to cultivate mathematical proficiency in the classroom. Accompanied by comprehensive guides and readily available answers, instructors can focus on mentoring and nurturing their students, secure in the knowledge that these books provide a robust framework for effective learning.

Within the pages of Summer Bridge Building Activities books lies not just the promise of academic excellence, but the seeds of a brighter future. By integrating these resources into your child's summer routine, you are bestowing upon them the gifts of confidence, curiosity, and a lifelong love of learning.

Invest in your child's future today with Summer Bridge Building Activities books — because every great journey begins with a single step, and this step can change everything. Keep the momentum of learning alive over the summer, and watch your child soar to new academic heights.

Contents

Equations (Two Sides)	1
Solving Two-Step Equations	5
Evaluating Equations	13
Solving Inequalities	20
Percent	30
Percent Word Problems	32
Ratio and Proportion Word Problems	37
Verbal Algebra	44
Simplify Expressions	51
Linear Equations	57
Find Slope from two Points	60
Graphing Linear Equations	63
System of Equations	68
Quadratic Equations	75

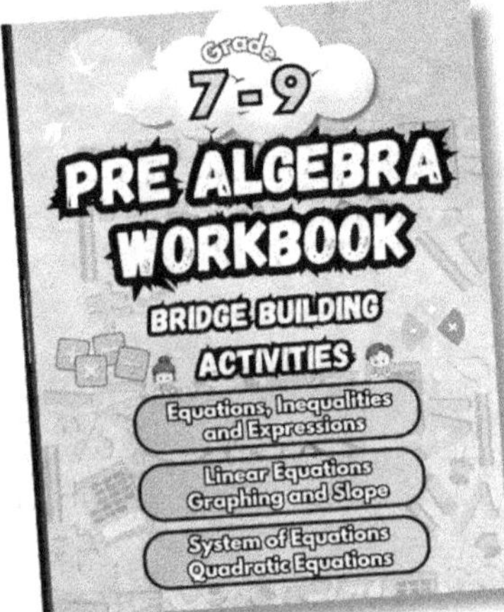

Grade
7 - 9
PRE ALGEBRA
WORKBOOK
BRIDGE BUILDING
ACTIVITIES
Equations, Inequalities
and Expressions
Linear Equations
Graphing and Slope
System of Equations
Quadratic Equations

Grade
6 - 8
PRE ALGEBRA
WORKBOOK
BRIDGE BUILDING
ACTIVITIES
Equations
One Side and Two Sides
Verbal Algebra
Expressions
Linear Equations and Slope
Order of Operations

Grade
5 - 6
PRE ALGEBRA
WORKBOOK
BRIDGE BUILDING
ACTIVITIES
Integers, Mixed Numbers
Decimals and Fractions
Place Value
Exponents and Roots
Percentage and Ratio
Word Problems

PRE ALGEBRA
WORKBOOK
for
Beginners
Integers
Fractions, Mixed Numbers
Place Value
Exponents and Roots
Percentage
Ratio Conversion

PRE ALGEBRA
WORKBOOK
for
Adults
Integers
Percent and Ratio
Equations, Inequalities
Expressions
Order of Operations

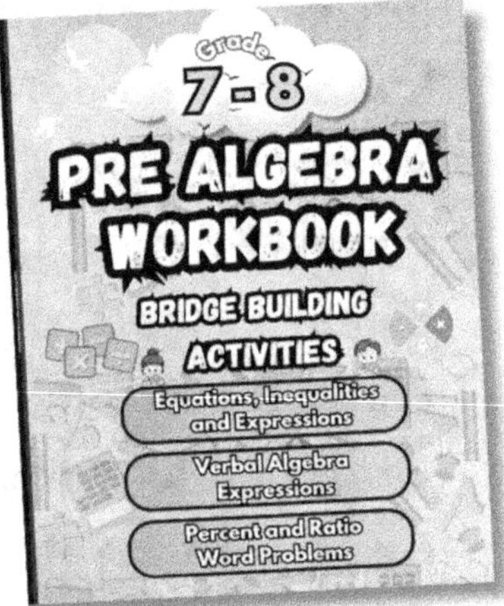

Grade
7 - 8
PRE ALGEBRA
WORKBOOK
BRIDGE BUILDING
ACTIVITIES
Equations, Inequalities
and Expressions
Verbal Algebra
Expressions
Percent and Ratio
Word Problems

Grade
9 - 10
PRE ALGEBRA
WORKBOOK
BRIDGE BUILDING
ACTIVITIES
Equations and Inequalities
Verbal Algebra
Linear and Quadratic
Equations
System of Equations
Polynomials

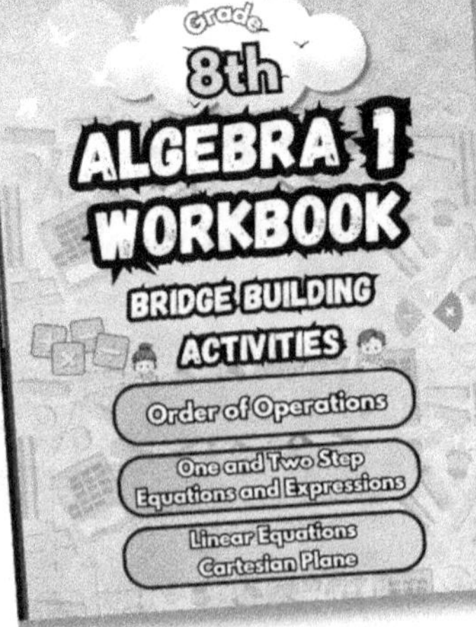

Grade
8th
ALGEBRA 1
WORKBOOK
BRIDGE BUILDING
ACTIVITIES
Order of Operations
One and Two Step
Equations and Expressions
Linear Equations
Cartesian Plane

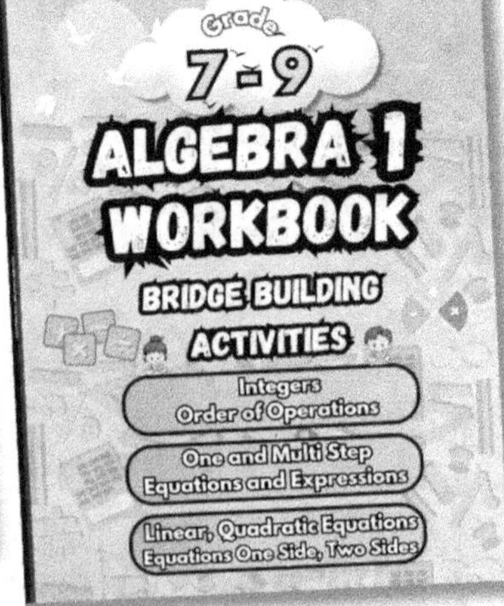

Grade
7 - 9
ALGEBRA 1
WORKBOOK
BRIDGE BUILDING
ACTIVITIES
Integers
Order of Operations
One and Multi Step
Equations and Expressions
Linear, Quadratic Equations
Equations One Side, Two Sides

Equations (Two Sides)

A two-sided equation is an equation where both sides have expressions with variables and constants. The goal when solving a two-sided equation is to find the value of the variable that makes both sides equal.

For example: Let's solve an equation:
$$9 + 8x + 8 = 64 + x + 2$$

- Combine Like Terms: Simplify each side of the equation by combining like terms (terms with the same variable or constants).
$$9 + 8x + 8 = 64 + x + 2$$
$$17 + 8x = 66 + x$$

- Isolate the Variable: Use inverse operations to isolate the variable on one side of the equation.

subtract x from both sides:
$$17 + 8x - x = 66 + x - x$$
$$17 + 7x = 66$$

subtracting 17 from both sides:
$$17 - 17 + 7x = 66 - 17$$
$$7x = 49$$

divide both sides by 7:
$$\frac{7x}{7} = \frac{49}{7} = x = 7$$

- Check Solution: Once you find the solution, substitute it back into the original equation to ensure it makes the equation true.

Substitute $x = 7$ back into the original equation:
$$9 + 8(7) + 8 = 64 + 7 + 2$$
$$9 + 56 + 8 = 64 + 7 + 2$$
$$73 = 73$$

Equations (Two Sides)

Solve for the variable.

1) $3 + 2z = 12 - z$

2) $4z + 8 = 53 - z$

3) $3 + 4k + 4 = 40 + k + \text{-}6$

4) $33 + 2m = 7m + 3$

5) $82 - 6y = 4 + 7y$

6) $4k = 35 - k$

7) $48 + y + 2 = 6 + 6y + 9$

8) $5x + 1 = 8 + 4x$

9) $4k + 24 = 8 + 8k$

10) $8y = 56 + y$

11) $3y = 14 + y$

12) $5x = 4 + x$

13) $10 + y = 2y + 2$

14) $7 + 7z = 23 - z$

15) $2 + 4m + 2 = 14 - m$

16) $8 + k = 2k$

17) $6 - z = 2z$

18) $24 - m + 14 = 7 + 3m + 3$

19) $8 + x = 3x$

20) $29 + y = 9 + 4y + 5$

21) $8k + 3 = 7k + 8$

22) $8 + y = 2y + 7$

23) $17 + x = 2 + 4x$

24) $13 - k + 9 = 8 + 8k + 5$

25) $7 + 2k + 4 = 14 + k$

26) $21 - x = 9 + 2x + 3$

27) $34 + m + 1 = 5 + 8m + 2$

28) $8 + 5x + 6 = 30 + x$

29) $15 + z = 4 + 4z + 8$

30) $7 + 3m + 3 = 26 - m$

31) $2m + 29 = 5m + 5$

32) $15 - k = 4k$

33) $3 + 5x = 9 - x$

34) $15 - z = 3 + 5z$

35) $7k + 9 = 90 - 2k$

36) $2 + y = 2y + 1$

37) $1 + 5m + 4 = 13 + m$

38) $9y + 4 = 6y + 13$

Solving Two-Step Equations

Solving two-step equations involves finding the value of the variable that makes the equation true. In a two-step equation, two operations (addition, subtraction, multiplication, or division) are performed on the variable.

The goal is to isolate the variable on one side of the equation by performing inverse operations in the reverse order of operations.

For example:

Given the equation $18 = (10 + b) - 2$, where we want to solve for b.

To solve for b, we need to undo the operations that have been performed on b.

1. Undo the subtraction by adding 2 to both sides:

$$18 + 2 = (10 + b) - 2 + 2$$
$$20 = 10 + b$$

2. Undo the addition by subtracting 10 from both sides:

$$20 - 10 = 10 + b - 10$$
$$10 = b$$

So, the solution to the equation is $b = 10$

Let's substitute $b = 10$ back into the original equation to verify if it satisfies the equation:

Original equation:

$$18 = (10 + b) - 2:$$

Substitute $b = 10$:

$$18 = (10 + 10) - 2$$

simplify:

$$18 = 20 - 2$$
$$18 = 18$$

Since the equation simplifies to $18 = 18$, it confirms that our solution $b = 10$ is correct.

Solving Two-Step Equations

Solve for the variable.

1) $55 = (10 + x) \cdot 5$

2) $66 = (7 \cdot m) + 3$

3) $32 = (8 \cdot z) + 8$

4) $44 = 4 \cdot (7 + x)$

5) $9 = 4y + 5 + (3y - 3)$

6) $x + 9x + 9x = 190$

7) $4m + 7 = 27$

8) $100 = 9z + 10$

9) $19 = 3x + 10$

10) $7s + 3s - 6 = 4$

11) $(8m)^2 = 576$

12) $(10 \cdot m) - 3 = 7$

13) $41 = 7 + (4z + 6)$

14) $1{,}296 = (6z)^2$

15) $5 + (4 \cdot s) = 45$

16) $7z + 9z - 8 = 120$

17) $(1 - a) \cdot 1 = -1$

18) $k + 6 + 8k = 69$

19) $9 \cdot (10 - a) = 54$

20) $5a - 8 + 8a = 5$

21) $-49 = 7 \cdot (2 - m)$

22) $3k - 3 + 2k = 7$

23) $65 = (9 + m) \cdot 5$

24) $83 = 2 + (9 \cdot z)$

25) $1 \cdot (4 - z) = -2$

26) $b + 6 + 6b = 76$

27) $1 \cdot (10 - k) = 9$

28) $11 = b + 5 + 2b$

29) $8 - (3 \cdot a) = -1$

30) $4 \cdot (4 - y) = -20$

31) $7 \cdot (8 + y) = 119$

32) $36 = (10 - m) \cdot 6$

<u>**Evaluating Equations**</u>

Evaluating expressions involves substituting given values for variables in an expression and then performing the indicated operations to find the result.

For example: Let's evaluate $4x - 10$, when $x = 3$:

Step 1: Substitute the given value for the variable:

Replace every occurrence of x in the expression $4x - 10$ with the given value, which is 3:

$$= 4(3) - 10$$

Step 2: Perform the operations:

Perform the indicated operations according to the order of operations (PEMDAS - Parentheses, Exponents, Multiplication and Division, Addition and Subtraction):

$$= 4 \times 3 - 10$$

Step 3: Simplify:

Calculate the result:

$$12 - 10 = 2$$

Evaluating Equations

Evaluate each expression when: $x = 2$

1) $(8 \cdot x) + 8x - 8 =$

2) $x \cdot 8 + 8 =$

3) $x(8 + x) =$

4) $(5x + 10) + (10x - 8) =$

5) $9x + 7 =$

6) $(6x + 3) \cdot (x - 10) =$

7) $8 + (x - 9)(x) =$

8) $x + (x \cdot 9) =$

9) $2x^1 + 8x^1 =$

10) $3 + x(10 - x) + 8x =$

Evaluating Equations

Evaluate each expression when: x = 1

1) $2(9 + x) + 8x - 10 =$

2) $8 \cdot x =$

3) $10x - x =$

4) $2 - (7 \cdot x) =$

5) $7x + 10 \cdot (x + 8) - 10 =$

6) $7 + x =$

7) $(9 \cdot x) - 1 =$

8) $(3x + 2)(6x + 6) =$

9) $5x + 8 =$

10) $(10 + x) \cdot 1 =$

Evaluating Equations

Evaluate each expression when: x = 6

1) $9 + (1 \cdot x) =$

2) $(2x + 1) \cdot (x - 3) =$

3) $6 + (7x - x)(4 + x) =$

4) $x \cdot (9 - x) =$

5) $(10x + 2) \cdot (x + 5) =$

6) $6 \cdot x + x =$

7) $9x + x =$

8) $1 \cdot (4 + x) =$

9) $7(5x - 1) + 6(5 + x) =$

10) $10 + (x - 7) =$

SUMMER ALGEBRA WORKBOOK
BUILDING ACTIVITIES

Evaluating Equations

Evaluate each expression when: $x = 2$

1) $2 + (x \div 2) =$

2) $x \div 2 =$

3) $2x - 4 =$

4) $3(4x - 4) + 9(9 + x) =$

5) $(5x + 2)(9x + 8) =$

6) $4x + 10x - 5 =$

7) $(9 + x)(10x - 3) =$

8) $7(9 + x) =$

9) $10x + 10 =$

10) $9x + 2 =$

Evaluating Equations

Evaluate each expression when: $x = 6$

1) $6x - 10 =$

2) $9 + (x - 8) =$

3) $(6x + 10) \cdot (x + 6) =$

4) $x \cdot 5 =$

5) $10 + (x \div 2) =$

6) $7 \cdot x + 10 =$

7) $(x \div 1) + x =$

8) $x \cdot 5 + 4 =$

9) $(2x + 1) \cdot (x - 3) =$

10) $x + 5 =$

Evaluating Equations

Evaluate each expression when: $x = 5$

1) $1 \cdot (x - 4) =$

2) $(5 \div x) + 10 =$

3) $(x \div 5) + x =$

4) $x + (10 \div x) =$

5) $7x + x =$

6) $x + 6 =$

7) $6(x + 6) + 8x =$

8) $(6x + 5) \cdot (x - 2) =$

9) $5 + (2x - x)(3 + x) =$

10) $1(9x - 3) + 3(9 + x) =$

Summer Algebra Workbook — Building Activities

Evaluating Equations

Evaluate each expression when: $x = 5$

1) $2(x + 4) + x(9 - x) =$

2) $x + 6 \cdot (x - 5) =$

3) $(x^1 + 9) - 10(5 + x) =$

4) $9x + 8 \cdot (x + 1) - 2 =$

5) $x^1 + x - 5 =$

6) $3x + 8 \cdot (x - 8) =$

7) $4 + 6x - (7 + x) =$

8) $1 + (5x + 10) =$

9) $10x + 4 \cdot (x + 4) - 2 =$

10) $(2 - x) \cdot (4x + 8) =$

<u>**Solving Inequalities**</u>

Inequalities are mathematical expressions that compare the relative sizes of two values. They are used to express relationships where one quantity is:

- "$<$" (less than),
- "$>$" (greater than),
- "$<=$" (less than or equal to),
- "$>=$" (greater than or equal to),
- and "$\neq$" (not equal to) another quantity.

For example:

$$y + \text{-}10 \leq -8$$

To isolate y, we need to get rid of the constant term -10. Since -10 is being subtracted from y, we can undo this operation by adding 10 to both sides of the inequality:

$$y - 10 + 10 \leq -8 + 10$$

$$y \leq 2$$

To check the solution:

$$2 - 10 \leq -8$$

$$-8 = -8$$

The inequality is true when $y = 2$

Solving Inequalities

1)

$$0 \leq -6 - m$$

2)

$$\frac{z}{2} < -1$$

3)

$$-10 > k + -7$$

4)

$$4x < 6$$

5)

$$-21\,m \geq 12$$

6)

$$7 < \frac{z}{-1}$$

7)

$$3 < z - {-5}$$

8)

$$9 \leq 2 + k$$

9)

$$2 - y > 4$$

10)

$$2 > -6 + y$$

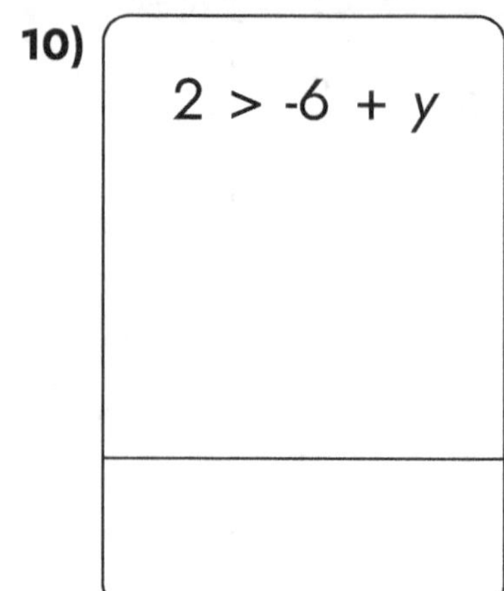

11)

$$-3 \geq \frac{x}{-5}$$

12)

$$-18\,z \leq -15$$

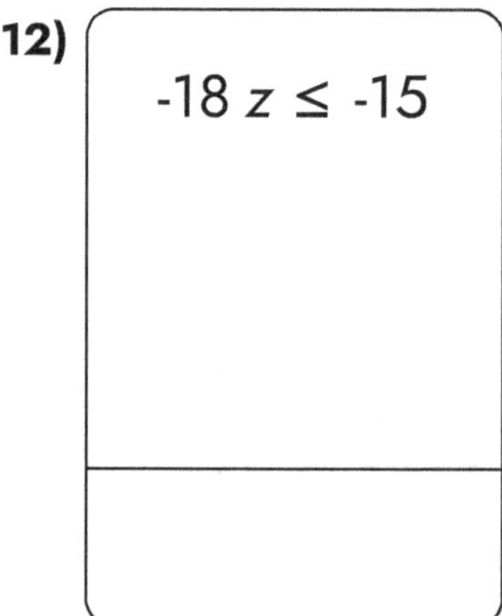

13)

$$-14x \leq 4$$

14)

$$\frac{z}{6} > -4$$

15)

$$x - 3 \leq 8$$

16)

$$2 + y > -4$$

17)

$$-1 - z > 1$$

18)

$$x + 5 > -8$$

19)

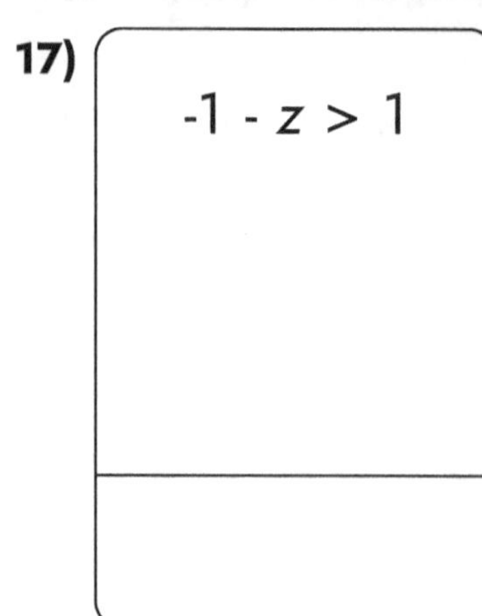

$$\frac{k}{4} > -2$$

20)

$$-4 > -6z$$

21)

$$3 \geq -9 + m$$

22)

$$3 - x > 9$$

23)

$$\frac{k}{3} \leq 5$$

24)

$$15 > 9x$$

25)

$$-3\,k \leq 12$$

26)

$$-7 > \frac{m}{2}$$

27)

$$y - -6 < -3$$

28)

$$z + -9 > -10$$

29)

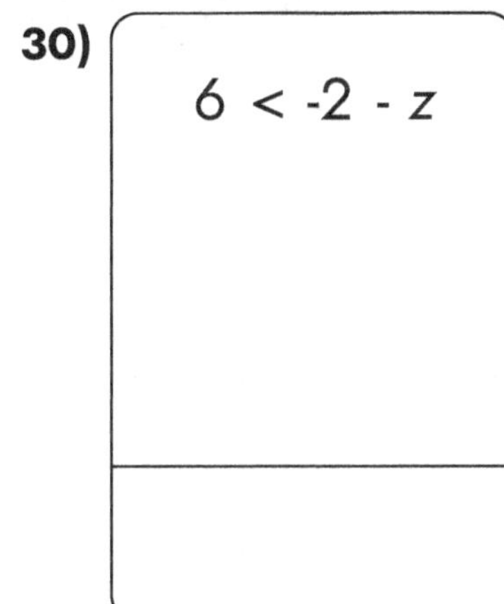

$$-2 > \frac{x}{2}$$

30)

$$6 < -2 - z$$

31)

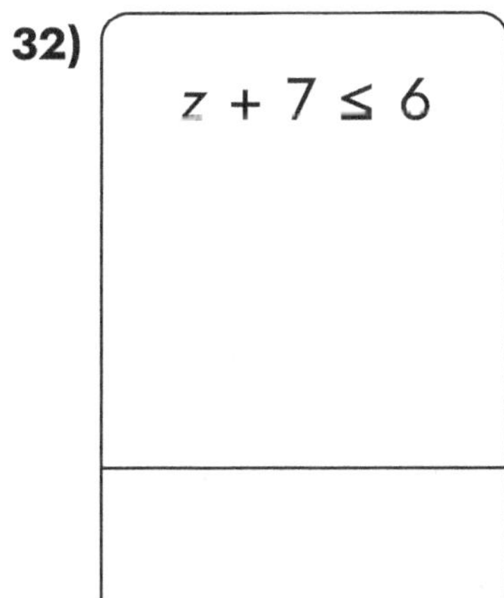

$$-4\,m < 3$$

32)

$$z + 7 \leq 6$$

33) 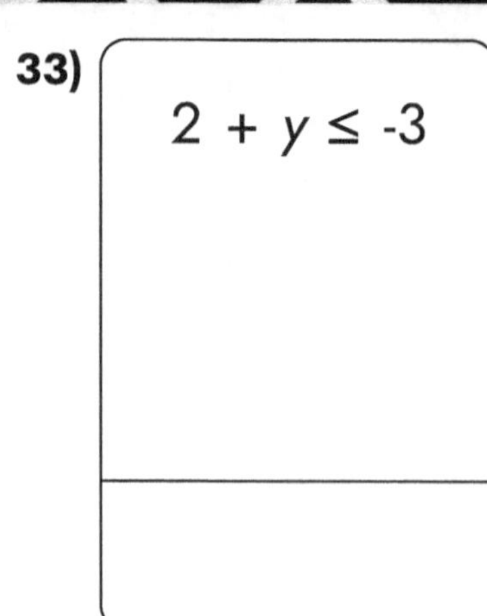

$$2 + y \leq -3$$

34)

$$-4 < \frac{m}{-8}$$

35)

$$-24 < -8m$$

36)

$$2 - z > 8$$

37)

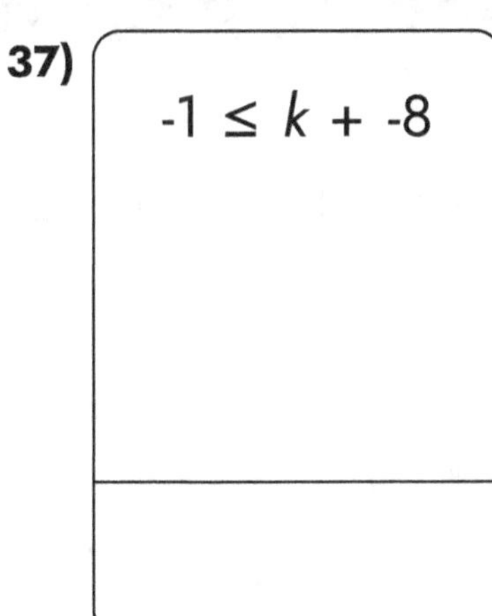

$$-1 \leq k + -8$$

38)

$$9 \geq x - -9$$

39)

$$10 < 2x$$

40)

$$-2 \leq \frac{k}{2}$$

Percentage

Percentage is a way of expressing a number as a fraction of 100. It is commonly used to represent proportions, rates, and comparisons. The symbol "%" is used to denote percentages.

To calculate a percentage, we multiply the given number by the appropriate fraction or decimal equivalent.

How to calculate a percentage:

Convert Percentage to Decimal: If the percentage is given as a percentage value (e.g., 25%), convert it to its decimal equivalent by dividing by 100.

$$\text{For example, 25\% as a decimal is } \frac{25}{100} = 0.25$$

Multiply: Multiply the decimal equivalent of the percentage by the given number. This gives us the portion of the number that represents the percentage.

$$100 \times 0.25 = 25\%$$

Result: The result is the calculated percentage value.

For example, to calculate 25% of 80:

Convert 25% to a decimal: 25% = 0.25.

Multiply 0.25 by 80: $0.25 \times 80 = 20$. The result is 20.

Percent

Calculate the given percent of each value.

1) 6.0% of 4 = ______

2) 48.0% of 2 = ______

3) 33.0% of 193 = ______

4) 0.8% of 8 = ______

5) 0.9% of 840 = ______

6) 25.0% of ______ = 72.75

7) 40.1% of ______ = 200.5

8) ______ of 632 = 4.424

9) 0.7% of ______ = 0.014

10) ______ of 411 = 3.699

11) [ ] of 2 = 0.664

12) 6.5% of [ ] = 38.155

13) 46.9% of 758 = [ ]

14) 7.3% of [ ] = 52.487

15) 4.2% of 49 = [ ]

16) 0.4% of [ ] = 0.272

17) 9.0% of [ ] = 14.13

18) [ ] of 4 = 0.156

19) [ ] of 60 = 5.64

20) [ ] of 39 = 2.886

Percent Word Problems

Percent word problems involve situations where percentages are used to calculate quantities or amounts. These problems often require converting percentages to decimals and then applying them to the given values.

For example:

Bella bought a pair of shoes for $90.00. If she paid an additional 90% for taxes, how much in total did she pay for the shoes?

- Bella bought a pair of shoes for $90.00.
- She paid an additional 90% for taxes.

Calculate 90% of $90:

$$Tax = 90\% \times 90$$

$$Tax = 0.90 \times 90$$

$$Tax = \$81$$

Add the tax amount to the original price:

$$Total\ cost = \$90 + \$81$$

$$Total\ cost = \$171$$

Percent Word Problems

1) A school has a total of 100 teachers. If 2% of them are men, how many male teachers are there?

2) If the number 75 is decreased by 8%, what is the value of the new number?

3) In a class of 100 students, 3% of them are in the Math Club. How many students are in the Math Club?

4) A restaurant makes a pizza that is 100 inches in diameter. If they want to increase the size of the pizza by 3%, what will be the new diameter?

5) Kai bought a bicycle that cost $75.00 when it was new. If he eventually sold it for 4% of the original cost, how much was it sold for?

6) Victoria bought maps for $100.00. If she paid an additional 35% for sales tax, how much in total did she pay for the maps?

7) Hannah bought a shoes for $50.00. If she paid an additional 6% for sales tax, how much in total did she pay for the shoes?

8) Vincent had 50 phones. He gave away 4% of them. How many did he have left?

9) A school has a total of 80 teachers. If 35% of them are men, how many female teachers are there?

10) A car dealership sold 50 cars last month. If the sales increased by 8% this month, how many cars did they sell this month?

11) A school has 25 students. If 16% of them play baseball, how many students play baseball?

12) A classroom has 25 students, of which 4% are girls. How many boys are in the classroom?

13) A store is having a sale where everything is 35% off. The medicines originally priced at $20.00 is now on sale. How much is the new price of medicines now?

14) Gemma bought a bag for $60.00. If she paid an additional 5% for sales tax, how much in total did she pay for the bag?

15) A store offers a 16% discount on all items. If Ava buys radios originally priced at $50.00, how much money did she save?

16) What is 62% of 50?

17) Joshua earned $80.00 for a week's work. If he paid 5% of it in taxes how much did he pay in taxes?

18) A store offers 4% discount on all products. If the sale price of shoes was 50, what was the original price?

19) A store has 100 shampoos. If 79% of them are sold at the end of the day, how many shampoos are sold?

20) In a survey of 50 people, 8% said they preferred android OS. How many people preferred android OS?

Ratio and Proportion Word Problems

We can use the concept of proportionality in solving many word problems, for example:

If a car travels 620 miles in six hours, how far can it travel in 12 hours?

Since the car travels a certain distance in a certain amount of time, we can assume that the distance traveled is directly proportional to the time taken.

Let d be the distance the car can travel in 12 hours.

We can set up a proportion:

$$\frac{\text{Distance1}}{\text{Time1}} = \frac{\text{Distance2}}{\text{Time2}}$$

Substituting the given values:

$$\frac{620 \text{ miles}}{6 \text{ hours}} = \frac{d}{12 \text{ hours}}$$

Now, let's solve for d:

$$d = \frac{620 \times 12}{6} = \frac{7440}{6} = 1240$$

So, the car can travel 1240 miles in 12 hours.

Ratio and Proportion Word Problems

1) A road is 140 miles long and it takes a car three hour to travel the entire length. What is the speed of the car in miles per hour?

2) A rectangular pool has an area of 464 square meters and a width of 10 meters. What is the length of the pool?

3) If a recipe calls for five cups of sugar for every 10 cups of flour, how many cups of sugar are needed for 23 cups of flour?

4) A train travels 153 miles in four hours. How far can it travel in eight hours?

5) If a square has an area of 119 square meters, what is the length of each side of the square?

6) If nine workers can build a house in 19 hours, how many workers are needed to build the house in six hours?

7) If 10 workers can complete a job in 12 days, how many workers are needed to complete the job in six days?

8) A charity received a donation of $4,581 from a company. If the donation was divided among five charities in the ratio 2:3:4:5:6, how much did the fourth charity receive?

9) A zoo has a ratio of four monkeys to every six lions. If there are 34 lions in the zoo, how many monkeys are there?

10) A recipe calls for four cups of sugar for every seven cups of flour. If you have 16 cups of flour, how much sugar is needed?

11) A bus travels at a speed of 83 miles per hour. How long will it take to travel 171 miles?

12) A train travels 167 miles in four hours. How far can it travel in 15 hours?

13) A grocery store has a ratio of two apples to every 10 oranges. If there are 36 oranges in the store, how many apples are there?

14) If a recipe calls for two cups of water for every four cups of rice, how much water is needed for seven cups of rice?

15) If a team of three construction workers can build a road in nine days, how many workers are required to complete the road in eight days?

16) A farmer has a ratio of five sheep to every 10 cows in his pasture. If there are 41 cows in the pasture, how many sheep are there?

17) A car can travel 56 miles per gallon of gas. How many gallons of gas are needed to travel 146 miles?

18) In a bag of candies, the ratio of chocolate candies to fruit candies is four:nine. If there are 12 fruit candies, how many chocolate candies are there?

19) A car travels 156 miles in four hours. How far can it travel in seven hours?

20) A school has a ratio of four female teachers to every seven male teachers. If there are 30 male teachers, how many female teachers are there?

21) If six chefs can bake 100 cakes in 16 hours, how many chefs are needed to bake the same number of cakes in seven hours?

Verbal Algebra

1) Find two consecutive odd integers such that four times the larger decreased by the smaller is 17.

2) One of two numbers is eight more than the other. The sum of the numbers is 14. Find the numbers.

3) Thirty-six more than the second of three consecutive even integers is the same as the difference between the third and nine times the first. Find the numbers.

4) The greater of two numbers is 2 less than four times the smaller number. Their sum is 43. Find the numbers.

5) The sum of three consecutive numbers is 21. What are the numbers?

6) Three times the sum of a number and nine times the number is 180. Find the number.

7) Find two consecutive even integers such that three times the smaller decreased by the larger is 10.

8) The difference of a number and one is equal to 3. What is the number?

9) 35 is equal to the product of five and some number. Find the number.

10) Five times the difference of 13 minus a number is 40. What is the number?

11) The sum of two numbers is 18. One number is six less than the other. Find the numbers.

12) One number is four more than another number. The sum of the larger number and twice the smaller number is 19. Find the numbers?

13) The sum of a number and four is 13. Find the number.

14) One of two numbers is one-third of the other number. The sum of the numbers is 4. Find the numbers.

15) One of two numbers is one-half of the other number. The sum of the numbers is 9. Find the numbers.

16) One number is 7 more than another number. The sum of twice the larger number and six times the smaller is 86. What are the numbers?

17) Five more than ten times a number is 105. What is the number?

18) Find two consecutive even integers such that three times the smaller decreased by the larger is 14.

19) The sum of two numbers is 8. One number is four less than the other. Find the numbers.

20) Ten times the difference of 5 minus a number is 20. What is the number?

21) The sum of two numbers is 17. The difference of the same two numbers is seven. Find the numbers.

22) 3 is equal to the product of three and some number. Find the number.

23) Find two consecutive even integers such that four times the smaller decreased by the larger is 4.

24) The sum of two consecutive odd numbers is 16. Find the numbers.

25) When a number is divided by three, the result is 6. What is the number?

26) One less than twice a number is 9. Find the number.

27) One number is nine times another. Their sum is 60. Find the numbers.

28) One number is three more than another number. The sum of the larger number and twice the smaller number is 6. Find the numbers?

29) One less than a number is 2. Find the number.

30) The difference of a number and seven is equal to 8. What is the number?

31) The quotient of a number and four increased by 2 is 3. What is the number?

32) The quotient of a number and nine increased by 7 is 10. What is the number?

<u>**Simplifying Expressions**</u>

It involves combining like terms and performing operations to make the expression easier to understand and work with.

Let's simplify the expression:

$$2x - 2x + 8 + 4$$

- Combine like terms: First, we look for terms with the same variable and exponent. In this expression, $2x$ and $-2x$ are like terms, so they can be combined:

$$2x - 2x = 0$$

- Substitute the simplified terms: After combining the like terms, the expression becomes:

$$0 + 8 + 4$$

- Combine the remaining terms: Now, we add the constants together:

$$8 + 4 = 12$$

Simplify Expressions

1) $6 + 2y - 7y$

2) $3x + 11 + 5x + 18 + 10x + 15$

3) $15 + 4z - 15 + 9z - 10 + 6z$

4) $m + 5 + 17m$

5) $m + 18 + 15m$

6) $12z - 7 - 4z + 6$

7) $18z + 7 + 13z$

8) $6 + 13z + 9 + 13z$

9) $-20 - x + 15 - 17x$

10) $z - 2z$

11) $12 + 9z - 11 + 12z$

12) $11m + 8 - 6m + 20 + 11m + 5$

13) $14 + x - 5 + 9x$

14) $-8 + 20m + 2 - 9m$

15) $-2k + 16k + 19 - k$

16) $18 - 6z + 12 - 3z + 19 - 16z$

17) $13 + z + 15 + 13z$

18) $14y + 4 + 19y$

19) $-8 + 6x + 11 - 16x$

20) $-18m + 13 - 5m$

21) $16 + 17(-20m + 10)$

22) $11x - 12 + 12x - 14 + 19x + 2$

23) $y + 18y$

24) $-x - 9x$

25) $k - 14k$

26) $16 - 14k + 6 - 14k + 19 - 10k$

27) $15 + 12m - 9 + 5m - 20 + 11m$

28) $13y + 7 - 3y + 16 + 19y + 12$

29) $19 + 19(z + 14)$

30) $-z - 18z$

31) $15k + 11 - 2k - 15 + 4k - 20$

32) $-20z + 10z$

33) $4 - 1(-5x + 19)$

34) $4k + 7 - 14 - 9k + 10k$

35) $-6m + 10m + 14 - 3m$

36) $3 + 17x - 16 + 4x - 20 + 15x$

37) $13 + 20x - 4x$

38) $7k - 17 - 12k + 14$

39) $19 + 18(-19y + 15)$

40) $17m + 16 + m$

41) $17m + m$

42) $-y + 17y$

43) $-8z - 19 - 1 - 9z$

44) $12m + 3 - 6 - 14m + 6m$

45) $4m - 12 - 16m + 16$

46) $20m + 16 - 18m + 18 + 17m + 8$

Linear Functions

A linear equation is an algebraic equation that represents a straight line when graphed on a coordinate plane. It consists of variables raised to the power of 1 (i.e., no exponents higher than 1) and constant coefficients.

The general form of a linear equation in one variable x is:

$$ax + b = 0$$

Where a and b are constants, and x is the variable.

Let's solve the linear equation:

$$-2x + 9 = 5$$

- **Isolate the variable term:** We want to isolate the term containing x on one side of the equation. To do this, we'll move the constant term to the other side. Subtract 9 from both sides:

$$-2x + 9 - 9 = 5 - 9$$

$$-2x = -4$$

- **Divide by the coefficient of the variable:** To solve for x, divide both sides by the coefficient of x, which is -2:

$$\frac{-2x}{-2} = \frac{-4}{-2}$$

$$x = 2$$

Linear Equations

Solve for the variable.

1) $9y = -81$

2) $8x + 4 = 60$

3) $x = -6$

4) $-10y + (-9) = 71$

5) $-5(-2x - (-7)) = -105$

6) $-3y + (-3) = 9$

7) $-10(2x - (-3)) = 130$

8) $3(y - (-10)) = 21$

9) $-2x = -4$

10) $8y + 1 = 41$

11) $10y + (-2) = 8$

12) $8y + 0 = -8$

13) $6(-6y - (-5)) = 174$

14) $-1(-2y - (-1)) = -13$

15) $5x + 2x = 14$

16) $-2y - 3 = 15$

17) $x + 3x - 3 = -11$

18) $-9x + 0 = 36$

19) $x + (-5)x = -28$

20) $9x + (-5) = -41$

21) $2x + 5x = -63$

22) $-10x - 5 = 35$

23) $8y - (-8) = 8$

24) $5x + 4x = -36$

<u>**Slop from Two Points**</u>

The slope between two points on a Cartesian coordinate system is a measure of the steepness of the line connecting those points. It's calculated by finding the change in the y-coordinates divided by the change in the x-coordinates.

- The coordinates of the first point as $(x1 , y1) = (2,-30)$.

- The coordinates of the second point as $(x2 , y2) = (-5,40)$.

The formula to calculate the slope (m) between two points:

$$\frac{y2 - y1}{x2 - x1}$$

Find Slope from two Points

1) (17, -19) and (6 , 5)

2) (3, 2) and (-3 , 14)

3) (-8, -20) and (-11 , -1)

4) (-3, 17) and (11 , -15)

5) (-8, 16) and (-5 , -17)

6) (-12, 0) and (10 , 13)

7) (17, -1) and (-11 , -2)

8) (-20, 8) and (15 , 9)

9) (20, 15) and (8 , -12)

10) (7, 3) and (6 , -5)

11) (-8, -4) and (-2 , -18)

12) (5, -5) and (-11 , -13)

13) (8, 3) and (-8 , -18)

14) (-13, -7) and (20 , -3)

15) (-9, 13) and (8 , -17)

16) (-8, 19) and (14 , 4)

17) (-14, 1) and (0 , 2)

18) (-11, 2) and (-1 , 9)

19) (-10, -20) and (12 , 13)

20) (-19, 8) and (-13 , 2)

21) (-10, -18) and (11 , -2)

22) (-5, 12) and (1 , 6)

23) (16, -10) and (17 , 15)

24) (15, 2) and (-18 , -7)

<u>**Graphing Linear Equation**</u>

Graphing a linear equation involves plotting the points that satisfy the equation on a coordinate plane and connecting them to form a straight line. Linear equations are equations of the form $y = mx + b$, where m represents the slope of the line, and b represents the y-intercept, the point where the line intersects the y-axis.

To graph a linear equation:

1. Identify the slope (m) and y-intercept (b) from the equation.

2. Plot the y-intercept $(0,b))$ as a point on the y-axis.

3. Use the slope to find additional points on the line. The slope represents the change in y for every unit change in x.

4. Connect the points to form a straight line.

For example, to graph the equation:

$$y = \frac{9}{4}x - 8$$

1. **Identify the slope and y-intercept:** The slope is $\frac{9}{4}$, and the y-intercept is −8.

2. **Plot the y-intercept:** Plot the point $(0,-8)$.

3. **Use the slope to plot additional points:** the slop is $\frac{9}{4}$ to find another point. we will move up 9 units and 4 units to the right from the y-intercept to find another point.

4. **Draw the line:** Once we have at least two points, we can draw a straight line.

We can continue this process to plot more points and extend the line further if needed.

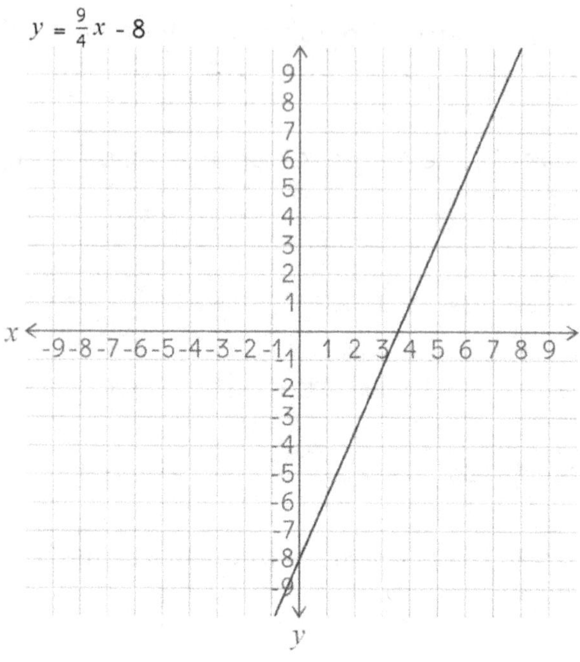

Graphing Linear Equations

1) 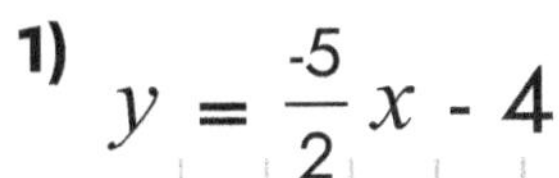
$$y = \frac{-5}{2}x - 4$$

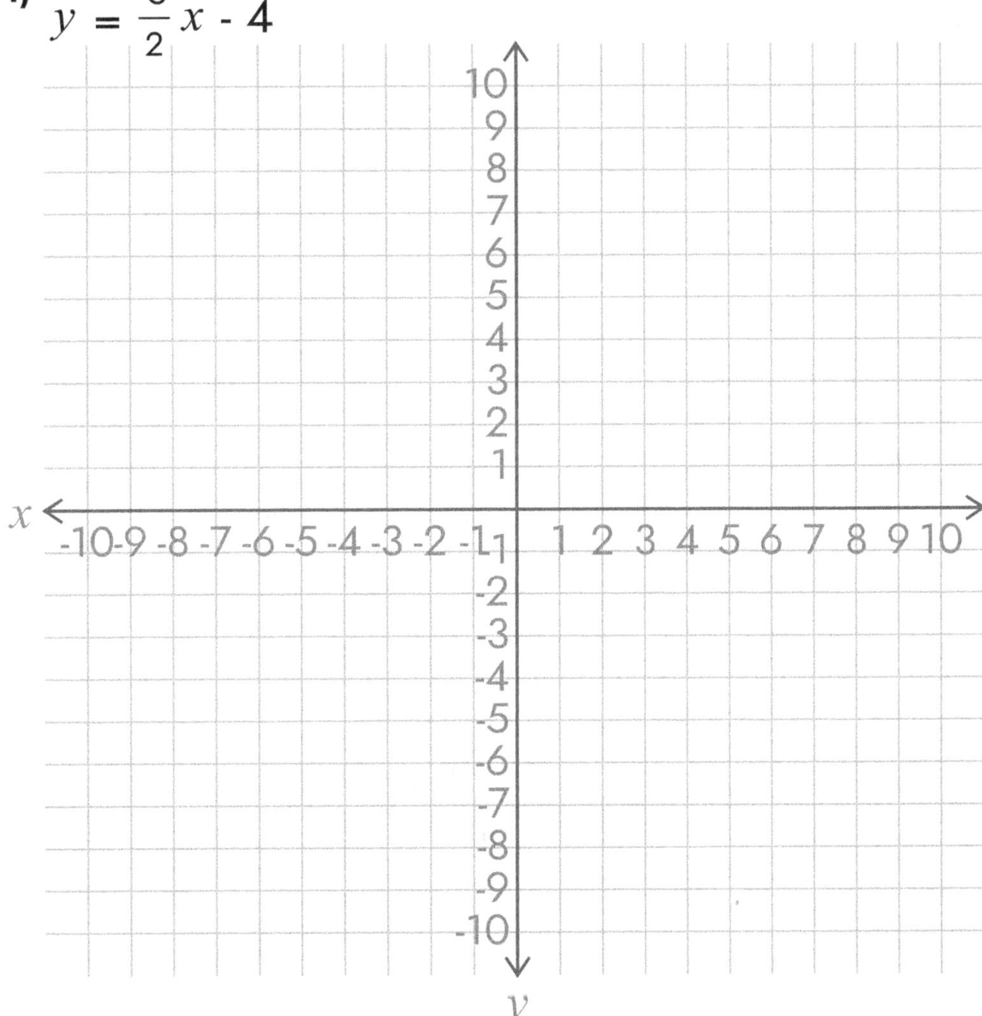

2) $y = \dfrac{-1}{2}x - 7$

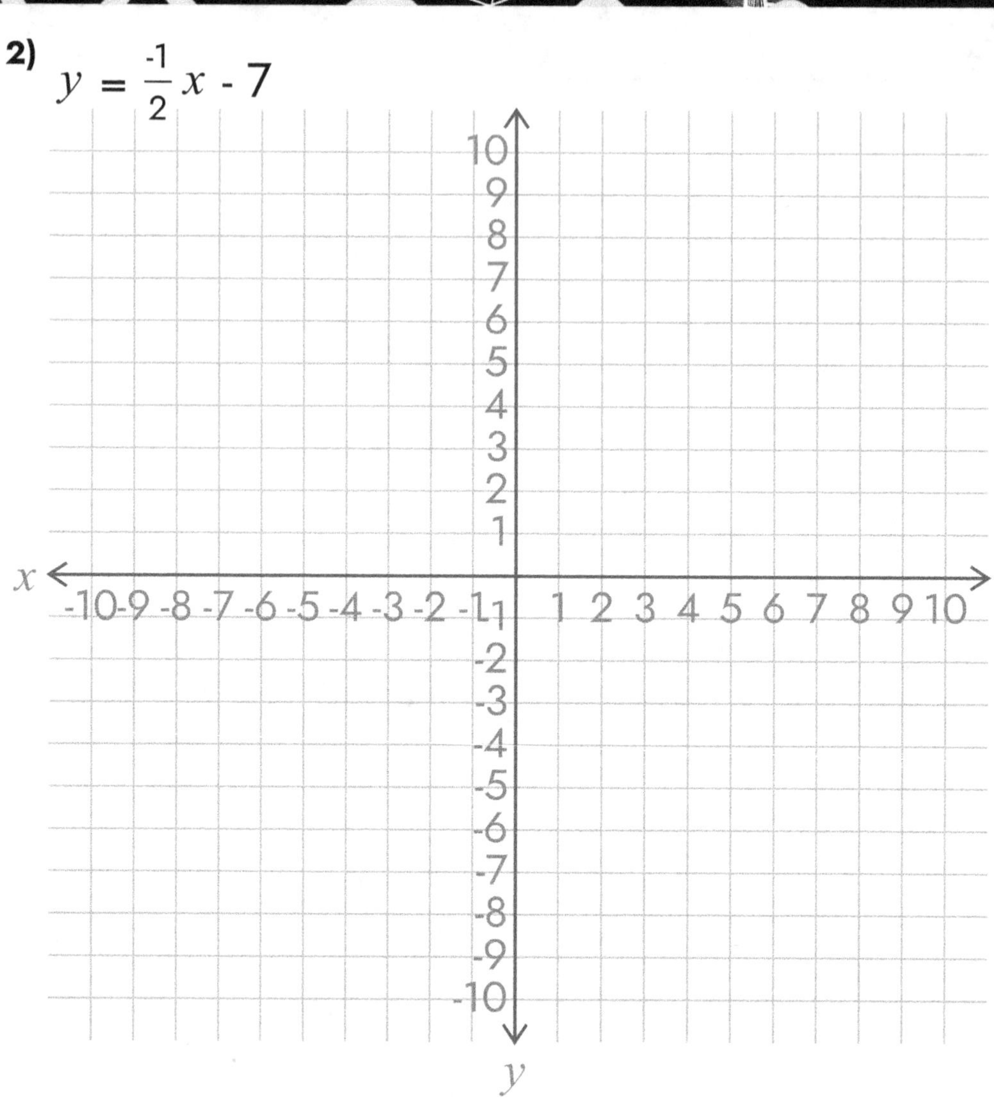

3)

$$y = -3x - 7$$

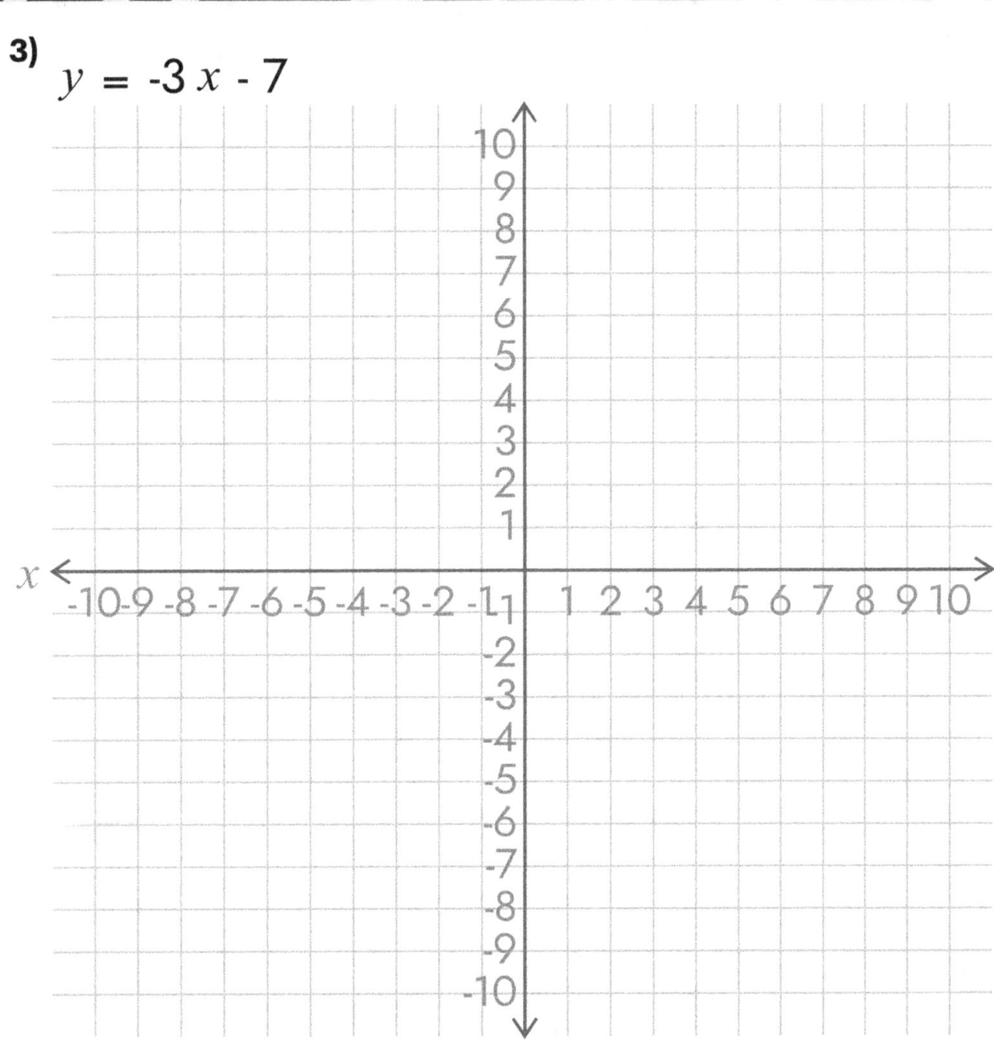

4) $y = -x - 9$

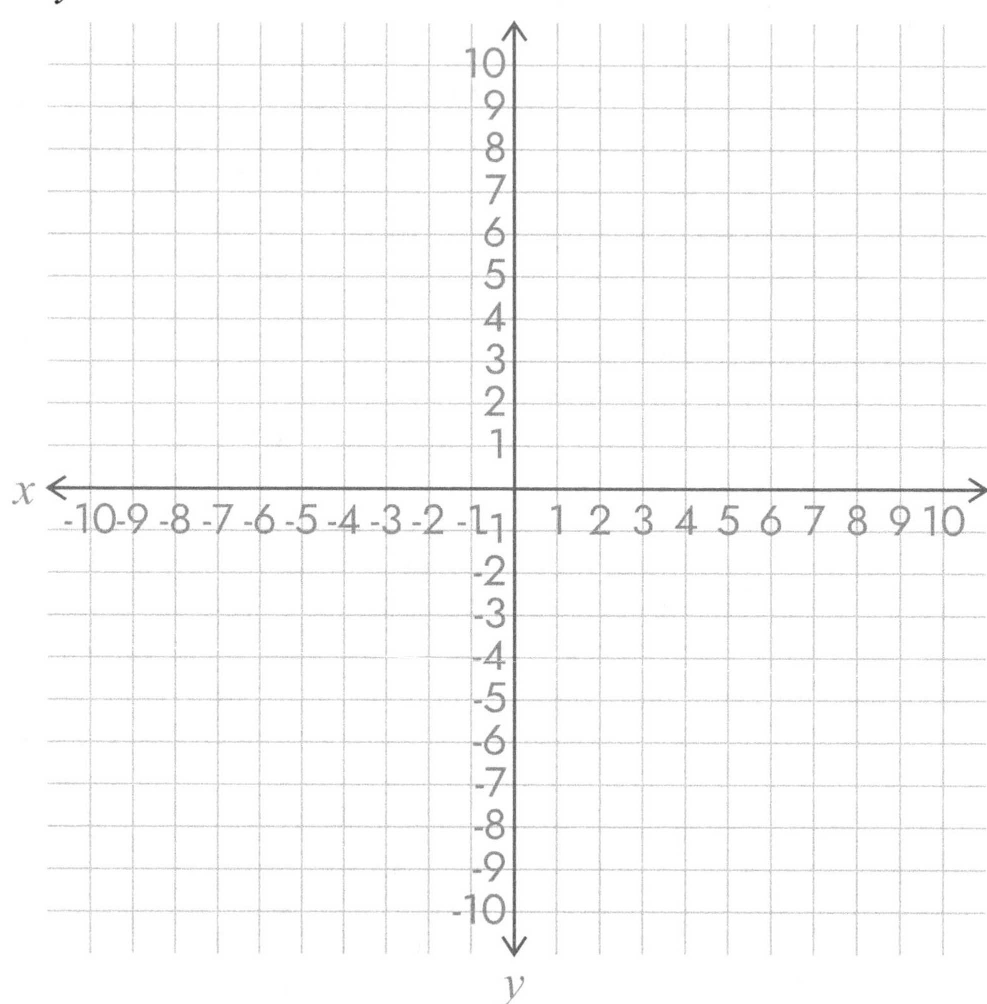

SUMMER ALGEBRA
WORKBOOK
NAME:
BUILDING ACTIVITIES

5)

$$y = \frac{1}{2}x - 7$$

10
9
8
7
6
5
4
3
2
1
x
-10 -9 -8 -7 -6 -5 -4 -3 -2 -1
1 2 3 4 5 6 7 8 9 10
-2
-3
-4
-5
-6
-7
-8
-9
-10
y

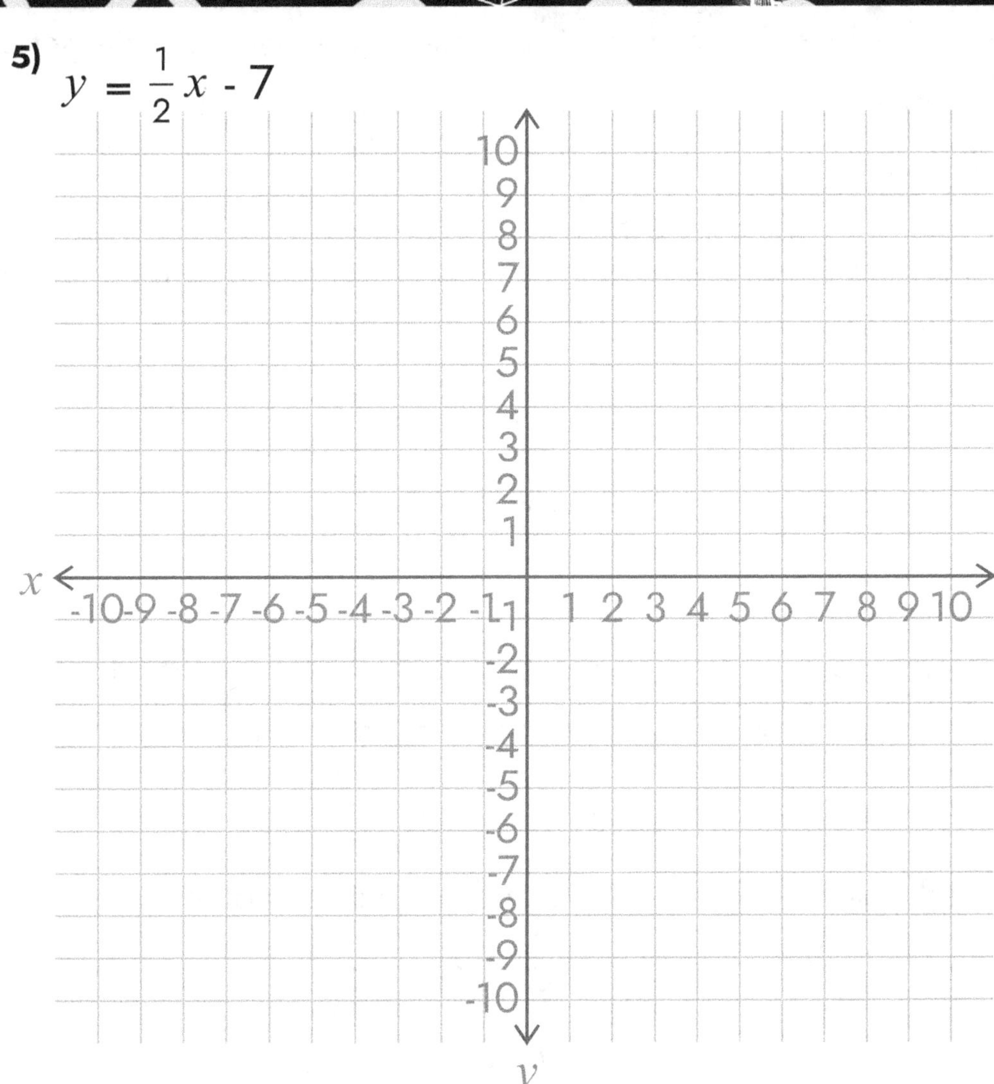

<u>**System of Equations**</u>

A system of equations is a collection of two or more equations involving the same set of variables. The solution to a system of equations is the set of values for the variables that satisfy all the equations simultaneously.

<u>**Solving by Elimination:**</u>

To solve a system of equations by elimination, we manipulate the equations to eliminate one of the variables.

Given the system:

$$4x + 5y = 6$$

$$10x + 6y = 8$$

Step 1: Multiply each equation by a constant such that the coefficients of one of the variables become equal or multiples of each other.

Let's try to eliminate the variable x.

- Multiply the first equation by 5 and the second equation by -2:

$$20x + 25y = 30$$

$$-20x - 12y = -16$$

Step 2: Add the two equations together to eliminate the variable x:

$$(20x - 20x) + (25y - 12y) = 30 - 16$$

$$13y = 14$$

Step 3: Solve for y:

$$y = \frac{14}{13} = 1.077$$

Step 4: Substitute the value of y into one of the original equations to solve for x. Let's use the first equation:

$$4x + 5\left(\frac{14}{13}\right) = 6$$

$$4x + \frac{70}{13} = 6$$

$$4x = 6 - \frac{70}{13}$$

$$4x = \frac{78 - 70}{13}$$

$$4x = \frac{8}{13}$$

$$x = \frac{2}{13} = 0.154$$

the solution to the system of equations is x =0.154 and y = 1.077.

System of Equations

1. $6x + 5y = 1$

$1x + 3y = 4$

2. $9x + 7y = 10$

$1x + 1y = 9$

3. $9x + 6y = 4$

$5x + 1y = 2$

4. $3x + 3y = 2$

   $10x + 6y = 6$

5. $5x + 6y = 7$

   $7x + 5y = 1$

6. $3x + 2y = 3$

   $1x + 8y = 2$

7. $8x + 10y = 6$

$1x + 7y = 3$

8. $3x + 9y = 3$

$5x + 8y = 3$

9. $1x + 7y = 9$

$4x + 2y = 4$

10. $7x + 9y = 2$

$10x + 9y = 3$

11. $5x + 3y = 10$

$4x + 6y = 8$

12. $10x + 6y = 3$

$4x + 8y = 9$

13. $1x + 8y = 2$

$4x + 10y = 10$

14. $9x + 6y = 9$

$5x + 4y = 6$

15. $1x + 1y = 3$

$10x + 6y = 6$

16. $1x + 8y = 4$

    $4x + 7y = 10$

17. $7x + 10y = 3$

    $8x + 5y = 9$

18. $2x + 10y = 6$

    $8x + 9y = 10$

19. 5x + 9y = 3

   7x + 2y = 8

20. 7x + 1y = 6

   8x + 4y = 3

Quadratic Equations

A quadratic equation is a polynomial equation of the second degree, meaning it can be written in the form:

$$ax^2 + bx + c = 0$$

where a, b, and c are constants, and x is the variable being solved for. The solutions to a quadratic equation are the values of x that make the equation true.

Now, let's solve the quadratic equation $11x^2 - 1 = 0$ and understand it step by step using quadratic formula.

1. Identify the coefficients:

   In the equation $11x^2 - 1 = 0$,

   $$a=11, b=0, \text{ and } c=-1.$$

2. Apply the quadratic formula:

   The quadratic formula states that for an equation $ax^2 + bx + c = 0$, the solutions for x are given by:

   $$x = \frac{-b \pm \sqrt{b^2 - 4ac}}{2a}$$

   Plugging in the values a=11, b=0, and c=−1 into the quadratic formula, we get:

   $$x = \frac{-0 \pm \sqrt{0 - 4(11)(-1)}}{2(11)}$$

3. Simplify inside the square root:

   $$0^2 - 4(11)(-1) = 0 - (-44) = 44$$

4. Plug in the simplified values:

   $$x = \frac{\pm \sqrt{44}}{22}$$

5. Simplify the square root:

   Since 44 is not a perfect square, we can write it as $\sqrt[2]{11}$

$$x = \frac{\pm \sqrt[2]{11}}{22}$$

6. Simplify further if possible:

   We can simplify $\sqrt[2]{11}$ to $\sqrt{11}$ by canceling out the common factor:

$$x = \frac{\pm \sqrt{11}}{11}$$

7. Final solution:

   So, the solutions to the equation are:

$$x = \frac{\sqrt{11}}{11} \text{ and } x = \frac{-\sqrt{11}}{11}$$

$$\text{or}$$

$$(x = 0.302, \text{ and } x = -0.302)$$

These are the roots of the quadratic equation. They represent the points where the graph of the quadratic equation intersects the x-axis.

Let's solve another equation:

$$-4p^2 + 6p - 6 = 0$$

$$p = \frac{-b \pm \sqrt{b^2 - 4ac}}{2a}$$

where $a = -4$, $b = 6$, and $c = -6$.

Let's plug these values into the quadratic formula:

$$p = \frac{-6 \pm \sqrt{6^2 - 4(-4)(-6)}}{2(-4)}$$

First, let's simplify inside the square root:

$$6^2 - 4\,(-4)\,(-6)$$

$$= 36 - 96 = -60$$

So, we have:

$$p = \frac{-6 \pm \sqrt{-60}}{-8}$$

We can simplify the square root of −60 by factoring out −1:

$$\sqrt{-60}$$

$$= \sqrt{-1 \times 60}$$

$$= \sqrt{-1} \times \sqrt{60}$$

$$= i\sqrt{60}$$

So, we have:

$$p = \frac{-6 \pm i\sqrt{60}}{-8}$$

Simplify:

$$\sqrt{60} \text{ to } \sqrt{4 \times 15} = 2\sqrt{15}$$

$$p = \frac{-6 \pm i \times 2\sqrt{15}}{-8}$$

Now, divide both the numerator and denominator by -2 to simplify:

$$p = \frac{3 \pm i\sqrt{15}}{4}$$

So, the solutions to the equation are:

$$p = \frac{3 + i\sqrt{15}}{4} \text{ and } p = \frac{3 - i\sqrt{15}}{4}$$

This equation $-4p^2 + 6p - 6 = 0$ has no real solutions.

When a quadratic equation has no real solutions, it means that the solutions are not real numbers, but rather complex numbers. In this case, the solutions involve the imaginary unit i because the discriminant ($b^2 - 4ac$) is negative, which results in taking the square root of a negative number when applying the quadratic formula.

In mathematics, such equations are said to have "no real roots" or "no real solutions." They are also sometimes referred to as having "complex roots" or "complex solutions." Complex numbers include a real part and an imaginary part, and they are often written in the form $a + bi$, where a and b are real numbers and i is the imaginary unit, defined as $i = \sqrt{-1}$.

Let's solve another equation:

$$12x^2 + 6x - 2 = 0$$

$$x = \frac{-b \pm \sqrt{b^2 - 4ac}}{2a}$$

where $a = 12$, $b = 6$, and $c = -2$.

Let's plug these values into the quadratic formula:

$$x = \frac{-6 \pm \sqrt{6^2 - 4(12)(-2)}}{2(12)}$$

First, let's simplify inside the square root:

$$6^2 - 4(12)(-2)$$
$$= 36 - (-96)$$
$$= 36 + 96$$
$$= 132$$

So, we have:

$$x = \frac{-6 \pm \sqrt{132}}{24}$$

Now, let's simplify the square root of 132:

$$x = \frac{-6 \pm \sqrt{4 \times 33}}{24}$$
$$x = \frac{-6 \pm 2\sqrt{33}}{24}$$
$$x = \frac{-6 \pm \sqrt{33}}{12}$$

So, the solutions to the equation are:

$$x = \frac{-6 + \sqrt{33}}{12} \text{ and } x = \frac{-6 - \sqrt{33}}{12}$$

or ($x = 0.229$, and $x = -0.729$)

Let's solve a quadratic equation where the right side is a number, instead of 0.

$$-8n^2 + 6n + 30 = 7$$

To solve the equation, we first need to bring all terms to one side to set the equation equal to zero:

$$-8n^2 + 6n + 30 - 7 = 0$$

Simplify:

$$-8n^2 + 6n + 23 = 0$$

Now, to solve for n, we can use the quadratic formula:

$$n = \frac{-b \pm \sqrt{b^2 - 4ac}}{2a}$$

where $a = -8$, $b = 6$, and $c = 23$.

Plugging these values into the formula, we get:

$$n = \frac{-6 \pm \sqrt{6^2 - 4(-8)(23)}}{2(-8)}$$

$$n = \frac{-6 \pm \sqrt{36 + 736}}{-16}$$

$$n = \frac{-6 \pm \sqrt{772}}{-16}$$

Now, let's simplify the square root of 772. We can factor out 4:

$$\sqrt{772} = \sqrt{4 \times 193} = 2\sqrt{193}$$

So, our equation becomes:

$$n = \frac{-6 \pm 2\sqrt{193}}{-8}$$

So, the solutions to the equation are:

$$n = \frac{-3 + \sqrt{193}}{-8} \quad \text{and} \quad n = \frac{-3 - \sqrt{193}}{-8}$$

or

$$(n = -1.362, \text{ and } n = 2.112)$$

Quadratic Equations

1. $2x^2 + 6x - 24 = 0$

4. $6n^2 + 2n - 9 = 0$

2. $-6p^2 - 11p + 2 = 0$

5. $-3p^2 + p + 20 = 0$

3. $-5x^2 - 6x + 32 = 0$

6. $-5b^2 + 4b + 1 = 0$

7. $-3p^2 + 4p + 64 = 0$

10. $2x^2 - x - 17 = 0$

8. $-4v^2 + 8v + 117 = 0$

11. $12m^2 - 8m - 9 = 3$

9. $2x^2 - 2x - 84 = 0$

12. $11x^2 + 9x - 13 = -9$

13. $-10n^2 + 9n + 23 = 12$

16. $-m^2 + 104 = 5m$

14. $11x^2 + 5x + 4 = 5$

17. $-9m^2 = -18$

15. $4x^2 - 78 = 3$

18. $6n^2 = 7n + 115$

ANSWERS

Page 1:   Equations (Two Sides)

1. z = 3 **2.** z = 9 **3.** k = 9 **4.** m = 6 **5.** y = 6 **6.** k = 7 **7.** y = 7

8. x = 7 **9.** k = 4 **10.** y = 8 **11.** y = 7 **12.** x = 1 **13.** y = 8 **14.** z = 2

15. m = 2 **16.** k = 8 **17.** z = 2 **18.** m = 7 **19.** x = 4 **20.** y = 5 **21.** k = 5

22. y = 1 **23.** x = 5 **24.** k = 1 **25.** k = 3 **26.** x = 3 **27.** m = 4 **28.** x = 4

29. z = 1 **30.** m = 4 **31.** m = 8 **32.** k = 3 **33.** x = 1 **34.** z = 2 **35.** k = 9

36. y = 1 **37.** m = 2 **38.** y = 3

Page 5:   Solving Two-Step Equations

1. 1 **2.** 9 **3.** 3 **4.** 4 **5.** 1 **6.** 10

7. 5 **8.** 10 **9.** 3 **10.** 1 **11.** 3 or -3 **12.** 1

13. 7 **14.** 6 or -6 **15.** 10 **16.** 8 **17.** 2 **18.** 7

19. 4 **20.** 1 **21.** 9 **22.** 2 **23.** 4 **24.** 9

25. 6 **26.** 10 **27.** 1 **28.** 2 **29.** 3 **30.** 9

31. 9 **32.** 4

Page 13:   Evaluating Equations

1. 24 **2.** 24 **3.** 20 **4.** 32 **5.** 25 **6.** -120 **7.** -6 **8.** 20 **9.** 20

10. 35

Page 14:   Evaluating Equations

1. 18 **2.** 8 **3.** 9 **4.** -5 **5.** 87 **6.** 8 **7.** 8 **8.** 60 **9.** 13 **10.** 11

Page 15:   Evaluating Equations

1. 15 **2.** 39 **3.** 366 **4.** 18 **5.** 682 **6.** 42 **7.** 60 **8.** 10 **9.** 269

10. 9

Page 16:   Evaluating Equations

1. 3   **2.** 1   **3.** 0   **4.** 111   **5.** 312   **6.** 23   **7.** 187   **8.** 77   **9.** 30   **10.** 20

Page 17:   Evaluating Equations

1. 26   **2.** 7   **3.** 552   **4.** 30   **5.** 13   **6.** 52   **7.** 12   **8.** 34   **9.** 39

10. 11

Page 18:   Evaluating Equations

1. 1   **2.** 11   **3.** 6   **4.** 7   **5.** 40   **6.** 11   **7.** 106   **8.** 105   **9.** 45

10. 84

Page 19:   Evaluating Equations

1. 38   **2.** 5   **3.** -86   **4.** 91   **5.** 5   **6.** -9   **7.** 22   **8.** 36   **9.** 84

10. -84

Page 20:   Solving Inequalities

1. $m \geq -6$ **2.** $z < -2$ **3.** $k < -3$ **4.** $x < 3/2$ **5.** $m \geq -4/7$

6. $z > -7$ **7.** $z > -2$ **8.** $k \geq 7$ **9.** $y > -2$ **10.** $y < 8$

11. $x \leq 15$ **12.** $z \leq 5/6$ **13.** $x \leq -2/7$ **14.** $z > -24$ **15.** $x \leq 11$

16. $y > -6$ **17.** $z > -2$ **18.** $x > -13$ **19.** $k > -8$ **20.** $z < 2/3$

21. $m \leq 12$ **22.** $x > -6$ **23.** $k \leq 15$ **24.** $x < 5/3$ **25.** $k \leq -4$

26. $m < -14$ **27.** $y < -9$ **28.** $z > -1$ **29.** $x < -4$ **30.** $z > -8$

31. $m < -3/4$ **32.** $z \leq -1$ **33.** $y \leq -5$ **34.** $m > 32$ **35.** $m > 3$

36. $z > -6$ **37.** $k \geq 7$ **38.** $x \leq 0$ **39.** $x > 5$ **40.** $k \geq -4$

Page 30:   Percent

1. 0.24   **2.** 0.96   **3.** 63.69   **4.** 0.064   **5.** 7.56

6. 291	**7.** 500	**8.** 0.7%	**9.** 2	**10.** 0.9%
11. 33.2%	**12.** 587	**13.** 355.502	**14.** 719	**15.** 2.058
16. 68	**17.** 157	**18.** 3.9%	**19.** 9.4%	**20.** 7.4%

Page 32: Percent Word Problems

1. 2	**2.** 69	**3.** 3	**4.** 103	**5.** $3.00	**6.** $135.00
7. $53.00	**8.** 48	**9.** 52	**10.** 54	**11.** 4	**12.** 24
13. $13.00	**14.** $63.00	**15.** $8.00	**16.** 31	**17.** $4.00	**18.** 52
19. 79	**20.** 4

Page 37: Ratio and Proportion Word Problems

1. 46.67	**2.** 46.4	**3.** 11.5	**4.** 306	**5.** 10.91	**6.** 28.5
7. 20	**8.** 1,145.25	**9.** 22.67	**10.** 9.14	**11.** 2.06	**12.** 626.25
13. 7.2	**14.** 3.5	**15.** 3.38	**16.** 20.5	**17.** 2.61	**18.** 5.33
19. 273	**20.** 17.14	**21.** 13.71

Page 44: Verbal Algebra

1. 3, 5	**2.** 3, 11	**3.** 6, 8, 10	**4.** 34, 9	**5.** 6, 7, 8	**6.** 6
7. 6, 8	**8.** 4	**9.** 7	**10.** 5	**11.** 12, 6	**12.** 9, 5
13. 9	**14.** 3, 1	**15.** 6, 3	**16.** 9, 16	**17.** 10	**18.** 8, 10
19. 6, 2	**20.** 3	**21.** 12, 5	**22.** 1	**23.** 2, 4	**24.** 7, 9
25. 18	**26.** 5	**27.** 6, 54	**28.** 4, 1	**29.** 3	**30.** 15
31. 4	**32.** 27

Page 51: Simplify Expressions

| **1.** $-5y + 6$ | **2.** $18x + 44$ | **3.** $19z - 10$ | **4.** $18m + 5$ |

5. 16m + 18   **6.** 8z – 1   **7.** 31z + 7   **8.** 26z + 15

9. –18x – 5   **10.** –z   **11.** 21z + 1   **12.** 16m + 33

13. 10x + 9   **14.** 11m – 6   **15.** 13k + 19   **16.** –25z + 49

17. 14z + 28   **18.** 33y + 4   **19.** –10x + 3   **20.** –23m + 13

21. –340m + 186   **22.** 42x – 24   **23.** 19y   **24.** –10x

25. –13k   **26.** –38k + 41   **27.** 28m – 14   **28.** 29y + 35

29. 19z + 285   **30.** –19z   **31.** 17k – 24   **32.** –10z

33. 5x – 15   **34.** 5k – 7   **35.** m + 14   **36.** 36x – 33

37. 16x + 13   **38.** –5k – 3   **39.** –342y + 289   **40.** 18m + 16

41. 18m   **42.** 16y   **43.** –17z – 20   **44.** 4m – 3

45. –12m + 4   **46.** 19m + 42

Page 57: Linear Equations

1. -9   **2.** 7   **3.** -6   **4.** -8   **5.** -7   **6.** -4   **7.** -8   **8.** -3   **9.** 2   **10.** 5

11. 1   **12.** -1   **13.** -4   **14.** -6   **15.** 2   **16.** -9   **17.** -2   **18.** -4   **19.** 7   **20.** -4

21. -9   **22.** -4   **23.** 0   **24.** -4

Page 60: Find Slope from two Points

1. -2.18   **2.** -2   **3.** -6.33   **4.** -2.29   **5.** -11   **6.** 0.59   **7.** 0.04

8. 0.03   **9.** 2.25   **10.** 8   **11.** -2.33   **12.** 0.5   **13.** 1.31   **14.** 0.12

15. -1.76   **16.** -0.68   **17.** 0.07   **18.** 0.7   **19.** 1.5   **20.** -1   **21.** 0.76

22. -1   **23.** 25   **24.** 0.27

Page 63: Graphing Linear Equations

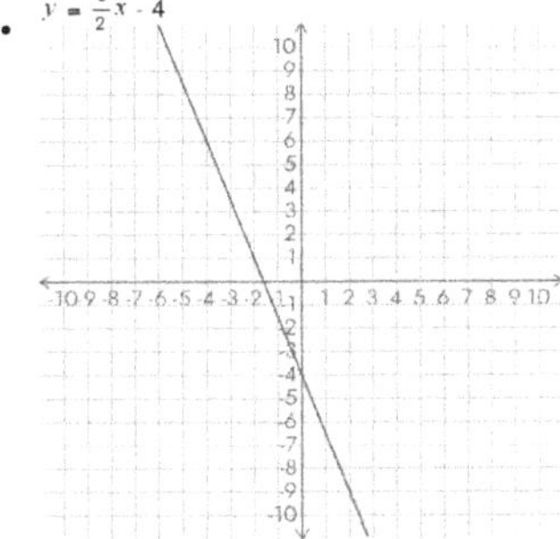

1. $y = \frac{5}{2}x - 4$

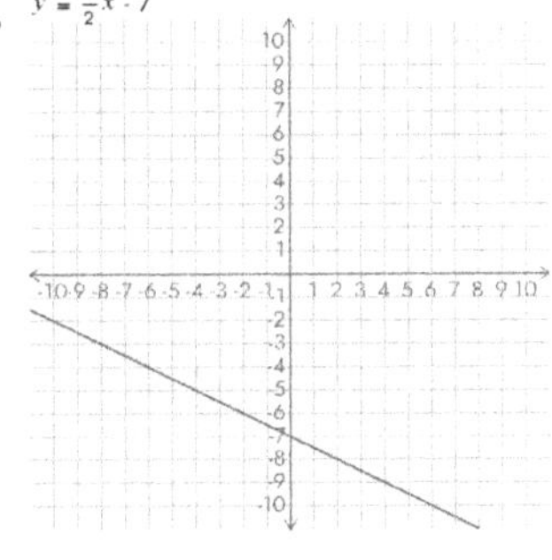

2. $y = \frac{1}{2}x - 7$

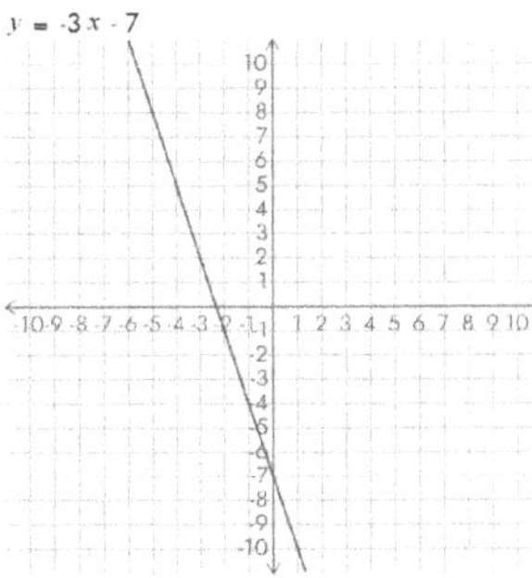

3. $y = -3x - 7$

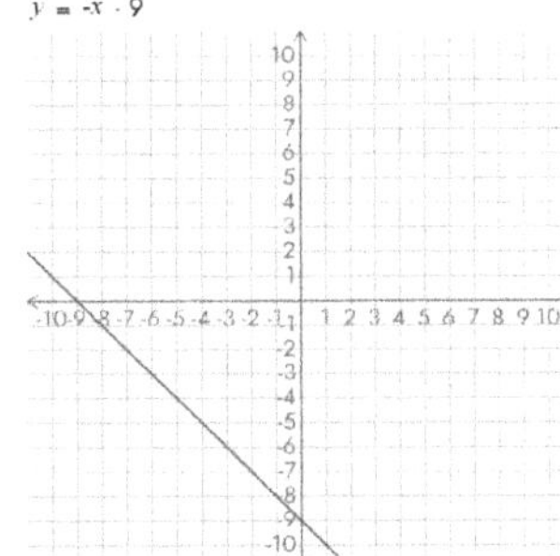

4. $y = -x - 9$

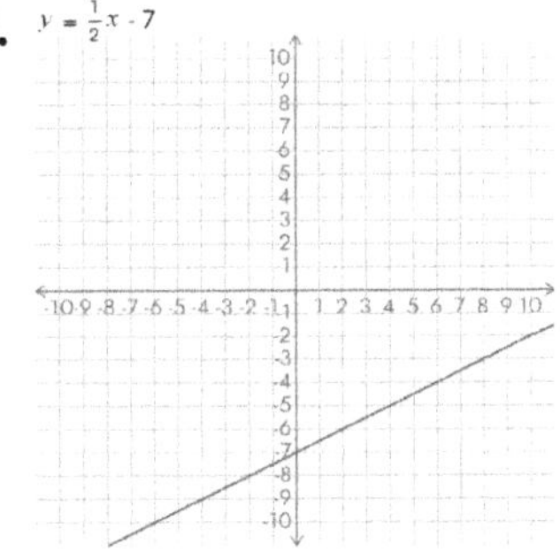

5. $y = \frac{1}{2}x - 7$

Page: 68 System of Equations

1. x = -1.31, y = 1.77
2. x = -26.5, y = 35.5
3. x = 0.38, y = 0.1
4. x = 0.5, y = 0.17
5. x = -1.71, y = 2.59
6. x = 0.91, y = 0.14
7. x = 0.26, y = 0.39
8. x = 0.14, y = 0.29
9. x = 0.38, y = 1.23
10. x = 0.33, y = -0.04
11. x = 2.0, y = 0.0
12. x = -0.54, y = 1.39
13. x = 2.73, y = -0.09
14. x = 0.0, y = 1.5
15. x = -3.0, y = 6.0
16. x = 2.08, y = 0.24
17. x = 1.67, y = -0.87
18. x = 0.74, y = 0.45
19. x = 1.25, y = -0.36
20. x = 1.05, y = -1.35

Page 75: Quadratic Equations

1. 2.275, -5.275
2. -2, 0.167
3. -3.2, 2
4. 1.069, -1.403
5. -2.421, 2.754
6. -0.2, 1
7. -4, 5.333
8. -4.5, 6.5
9. 7, -6
10. 3.176, -2.676
11. 1.387, -0.721
12. 0.32, -1.138
13. -0.691, 1.591
14. 0.15, -0.605
15. 4.5, -4.5
16. -13, 8
17. -1.414, 1.414
18. 5, -3.833